superstars!
superstars!
superstars!
superstars!

CREATIVE EDUCATION SPORTS SUPERSTARS

nadia
romaneci com

nadia
comane

neci comane

nadia comaneci

by Thomas Braun

photographs by Bruce Curtis

CREATIVE EDUCATION

Library of Congress Cataloging in Publication Data
Braun, Thomas, 1944-
Nadia Comaneci.

SUMMARY: A biography of the young Romanian who was the first gymnast to receive a
perfect score during Olympic competition.
1. Comaneci, Nadia, 1961-   —Juvenile literature.
2. Gymnasts—Romania—Biography—Juvenile literature.
[1. Comaneci, Nadia, 1961-   2. Gymnasts] I. Title.
GV460.2.C65B72   796.4'1'0924 [B] [92]   76-48955
ISBN 0-87191-592-8

nadia comaneci

nadia comaneci

On a bright summer day in 1976 the Queen of England royally stood up. Then two young Canadians carrying a torch ran into the stadium and lighted the traditional flame. Queen Elizabeth, speaking first in French and then in English, made an official-sounding declaration: "I declare open the Olympic Games of Montreal celebrating the XXI Olympiad of the modern era."

From somewhere among the 70,000 spectators a full orchestra struck up "O, Canada," and a parade of athletes representing 94 nations entered the Olympic Stadium. The parade was shorter than it might have been. Political bickering over some lofty international principles had caused many countries to withdraw their teams.

All of the contestants including a small teenager from Romania named Nadia Comaneci took their places in the infield. Together they repeated the Olympic oath pledging their best efforts "for the glory of sport and the honor of our teams." Hundreds of colorful flags were waved. Eighty homing pigeons — rented from their owner at five dollars apiece — were released. They drifted up and out of the large oval opening in the roof of the stadium and presumably flew home.

The spectacular global event called the Summer Olympics survived its first ordeal. It made it through its own opening ceremonies. Finally the real show was ready to begin. The TV cameras and the expert commentators had been turned on and warmed up. Over 8,000 newsmen were set to record all the drama about to be staged by the athlete-performers. And the Queen — temporarily the show's leading lady, tired from standing throughout the entire 90 minute ceremony — royally sat down.

As the opening ceremonies demonstrated, almost everything connected with the modern Olympics has become big, technically complex and very expensive. The stadium, built specially for the games, cost 685 million dollars. The Canadian government spent another 140 million dollars on security precautions for the participants. The rights to televise the competitions cost ABC Television 25 million dollars.

Technology made a large, new impact on the games. The Olympic flame was transmitted from Athens, Greece by means of a communications satellite and a laser beam. Other satellites were used to send TV coverage to more than one billion people around the world. For the running events in track and field, the starting blocks were wired to automatically detect a false start. In contests that depended on evaluation by judges, scores were fed into a computer and the results were displayed almost immediately.

Along with the various political debates, there were accusations of cheating. One judge claimed that he had been offered a bribe by another judge. A fencer was caught using an illegal device to score points on his opponent. Some contestants were eliminated for illegal drug use.

In the midst of the bigness and the many complications, the 14-year-old Romanian girl stepped forward and gave a series of gymnastics performances that easily cut through all the surface complexities. With each of her brief routines, Nadia Comaneci reminded her vast audience that the games still have a simple purpose: they provide an arena for athletic excellence.

By the end of the gymnastics competition, Nadia had collected five medals: three gold, one silver and one bronze. She also took first place in the "all-around" segment of the meet. But the accomplishment that created the most stir around the young girl was one of her early scores. She became the first gymnast in the long history of the Olympics to receive a 10.0 — a perfect score. Then as if perfect marks were as routine as forward somersaults, she rolled up six more.

Clearly the 1976 Summer Olympics had a new leading lady — a new little queen whose reign could not be challenged by any real monarch or by any other athlete at the summer games.

All of the Olympic gymnastics events took place at the Montreal Forum. Hockey is the sport usually played at the Forum. The large arena is the home of the Montreal Canadiens hockey team.

It would be difficult to find two sports with fewer similarities than hockey and gymnastics. Hockey is a fast and often brutal sport. During a game all of the players and fans focus their attention on the hard, black puck. In simple terms, the point of the game is to work together to get the puck into the opposing net as many times as possible before time runs out.

Gymnastics is very different. It is a much more individualized sport. Although teams do compete against each other, a team score is the total points earned by individual performers working alone.

For someone unfamiliar with gymnastics, a meet can be a very confusing experience. It lacks the focus and clear progression of a hockey, football or basketball game. In women's gymnastics each participant must perform in four areas: side horse vaulting, uneven parallel bars, floor exercise and balance beam. During a meet, action occurs in all four of these areas simultaneously. Women's gymnastics might best be described as a very polite four-ring circus.

Each of the four events has its own apparatus and demands specific, highly specialized skills. The main piece of equipment used in the side horse vault is the"horse" or padded, leather-covered hurdle. The horse is 44 inches high and 64 inches wide. A spring-type take-off board and a landing pad are also used.

The gymnast starts with a fast running approach between 60 and 80 feet in length. Using the take-off board she attains as much height as possible, makes contact with the horse using both hands, pushes off the horse and lands in a standing position on the mat.

The difficulty of a routine depends on the variations in body position — handstands, cartwheels, twists and somersaults — used during the vault.

The high bar of the uneven parallel bars (sometimes called asymmetric bars) is seven feet, six inches off the floor. The low bar is four feet, 11 inches high. Using many different swinging and soaring movements and changes in grip, the gymnast moves back and forth between the two bars in a continuous, rhythmic motion. Strong arms and shoulders are essential in this event. Often the dismount is the most spectacular part of the routine.

In some ways the floor exercise comes close to being a dance performance. It uses piano accompaniment and is performed on a large square mat. Lasting between one minute and one minute and 30 seconds, the routine incorporates tumbling, acrobatic and dance movements. Variations in tempo, rhythm and utilization of space are important elements of the exercise.

Some people consider the fourth piece of apparatus — the balance beam — to be the most difficult challenge in women's gymnastics. The wooden beam is four feet high, 16 feet long and only four inches wide. The gymnast mounts the narrow surface and executes a series of running and walking steps, leaps and jumps, dance movements, handstands, turns and even flips. The full length of the beam must be used to show the contestant's balance, precision and concentration.

A gymnastics meet is usually divided into two parts: compulsory routines and optional routines. In compulsories all participants in an event must perform the same routine. In the optional portion of the meet, the gymnast performs an individualized routine designed to show her own unique style and skills.

Scoring adds another complication to an understanding of gymnastics competition. Each routine is given a numerical score (10 is the highest possible mark) by each of four judges. The high and low scores are discarded and the average of the remaining two scores is awarded. Since all of this computation takes time, a meet is filled with the many suspenseful moments between the end of a performance and the announcement of the score.

Before the 1976 Olympic gymnastics competition began few people at the Forum, and even fewer in the huge television audience, had ever heard of Nadia Comaneci. At this point the most famous of all women gymnasts was Olga Korbut.

Prior to the 1972 Summer Olympics in Munich, Germany, women's gymnastics was as obscure an event as flat-water canoeing is today. But during the Munich games the world discovered Olga Korbut, and in the process, women's gymnastics became one of the most popular competitions of the Olympics. Millions of people watched and still remember Olga's up and down battle for gold medals in Munich.

Somehow the conditions were right in 1972 to make Olga Korbut the superstar of the Olympics. Along with Olga's fame came widespread interest in her sport. American young people saw Olga's dramatic performance on TV. Then many saw her in person when she later toured the United States with the Russian team. Suddenly gymnastics became the hottest new sport in America.

The people who closely followed women's gymnastics knew that Olga would be up against stiff competition in Montreal. Her teammate, Ludmilla Tourishcheva, was 23 years old and was nearing the end of her competitive career. Her last appearance in the Olympics would be in Montreal. Although Olga had received most of the attention in Munich, Ludmilla had

actually won the all-around event in 1972 and was considered to be the better gymnast. Many people thought that Ludmilla's age and experience would give her an important advantage over her younger rivals.

Then there was Nadia. Her name may have been new to the average spectator, but all serious gymnastics fans knew her well. Her career had been brief. Yet during her few years of competition she had won several of the most important international meets.

Nadia is a Romanian. She was born on November 12, 1961. Today she and her family live in the city of Gheorghe Gheorghiu-Dej, located about 200 miles north of Bucharest, the capital of Romania. Nadia's father is an auto mechanic and her mother works in an office. She has a younger brother Adrian. Her family lives in a new apartment complex not far from Nadia's school.

Like many Romanians, the Comanecis enjoy vacationing along the shore of the Black Sea during the summer. In the winter, snow covers the nearby Carpathian Mountains. When time permits, Nadia likes to ski. Another of her interests is collecting dolls. She also goes to the movies. Her favorite star is the French actor, Alain Delon.

Although Nadia appears to have all of the interests of a normal teenager, these activities are incidental to the time and energy she spends on her sport. In a way, Nadia's real family is her team, her real father is her coach and her life is a series of vaults, flips, twists and spins.

Bela Karolyi, the coach of the Romanian team, discovered Nadia when she was only six years old. He and his wife frequently scouted the Romanian kindergartens for new talent. One day he spotted two small girls playing outside during a recess period.

"They were running and jumping and pretending to be gymnasts," Karolyi remembers. "Then the bell rang, and they ran into the building and I lost them. I went into all the classes looking for them. I went again and still I couldn't find them. A third time I went in and asked, 'Who likes gymnastics?' In one of the classrooms two girls sprang up. One is now a very promising ballerina. The other is Nadia."

Karolyi took Nadia, her friend and several other children to a gym and gave each of them a simple test. They ran a 15-meter sprint, did a long jump and walked on the balance beam. "If they were afraid on the beam," adds the coach, "we send them home

right away. We only keep those who like it and show good balance.'' Nadia passed the test easily and began to train with her new coach.

One year later Nadia was the youngest gymnast in the Junior National Championships of Romania. In this first major contest, the seven-year-old finished in thirteenth place. Karolyi remembers giving Nadia a special reward, ''Because thirteen is an unlucky number, I bought her an Eskimo doll for good luck and told her she must never rank thirteenth again.'' Just one year later Nadia became the Junior National Champion.

By the time she was eight, Nadia was very serious about gymnastics. She began a rigorous training program and followed every detail of her coach's advice. She started a strict daily practice schedule. Nadia attends school for four hours each morning, returns home for a two-hour nap and then works out in the gym for three or four hours.

Height and weight are extremely important for a gymnast. Nadia is five feet tall and weighs about 85 pounds. To maintain her size and strength her diet is carefully controlled. She eats salads, fruit, milk and cheese. She avoids all sugar and bread.

During her long sessions in the gym, Nadia tries out new routines and polishes old ones. Karolyi uses a simple building-block teaching method. Every new move is divided into segments. Nadia begins with the easiest part, repeating it until she knows it perfectly. Then another, more difficult piece is added and so on until she can do the entire movement without even thinking about it.

The Olympics is not the only major international meet for gymnasts. The World Games gymnastics meet, also held every four years, was won in 1970 and again in 1974 by Ludmilla Tourishcheva. Nadia had already competed in several national meets but was not ready to try the World Games in 1974.

She was prepared, however, by the spring of 1975 to enter the European Championships in Skien, Norway. This meet is held every two years between the Olympics and the World Games. The European Championships is not a team competition. Each country (the United States is not invited) sends only two contestants. Also, only optional exercises are performed.

Because of an ankle injury Olga Korbut did not attend.

The two women representing Russia were Tourishcheva — considered the best gymnast in the world — and Nelli Kim. Romania sent Nadia and Alina Goreac.

During the workout period before the meet, spectators saw quickly that Tourishcheva would have to be very good to withstand the challenge from Comaneci. Ludmilla was the first up on the uneven bars when the contest started. She seemed nervous, made several errors and ended up with a 9.35. She almost fell on the balance beam and received a 9.25.

Nadia started out with an excellent floor exercise which included two double twists. Her mark was 9.65. In each of the remaining three events her scores were higher. By the end of the meet Nadia had won first place, Nelli Kim placed second and Ludmilla unhappily ended up in fourth place. By winning in her first appearance on the international scene, the 13-year-old Romanian became the newest, most exciting figure in women's gymnastics. Fans immediately started talking about a future match between Comaneci and Korbut. But they would have to wait.

In July, 1975, the Pre-Olympics were held in Montreal. This time neither Tourishcheva nor Korbut entered the meet. The battle for first place in the all-around category was again fought between Nadia and Nelli Kim. Comaneci narrowly won with a point total of 76.85. Kim's final total was 76.50.

Americans had their first chance to see Nadia in person when the Romanian team toured the United States in the early part of 1976. After a stop in Toronto, Canada, the Romanians competed in Tucson, Albuquerque, San Francisco and Denver. Nadia won every meet. In Toronto she scored six perfect marks out of a possible eight routines. No gymnast had ever before received more than a single 10 in an international contest.

The U.S. Olympic team manager, Rod Hill, saw Nadia perform in Tucson. "There are not enough words to explain the tremendous impact a gymnast such as Nadia Comaneci of Romania has on the sport," said Hill. "Nadia is in a class all her own . . . She could throw ten, twenty or thirty routines and score 9.8 or better in each of them. I have seen her throw six consecutive bar routines," Hill continued, "and hit every one of them and not be breathing hard. Her physical conditioning is fantastic."

After the last meet in Denver, Nadia went back to Romania. Then with only a four-day break, she returned to the United States to compete in the first annual American Cup meet held in New York City. Each participating country sent one male and one female gymnast. Again Korbut stayed home. The Russian entry was 14-year-old Yelena Davidova.

Over 10,000 people at Madison Square Garden watched Nadia score a 10 on her vault. Her scores were so high that she won the first day's all-around competition ending up two points ahead of the second-place finisher. On the second day in the finals she received another 10 in the floor exercise and once again finished with the highest combined score.

As the Summer Olympics approached, Nadia Comaneci had not lost a single international meet.

The Olympic gymnastics meet for women lasts four days. The first two days are devoted to team competition. The first day is set aside for compulsory routines and the second day for optionals. At the end of the team competition, the top team receives a gold medal and the top 36 gymnasts go on to compete for the individual all-around title on the third day. On the fourth and last day, six finalists enter each of the four events: vaulting, uneven bars, balance beam and floor exercise. Gold medals are awarded to the best woman in each of these four categories.

On Sunday, the day following the opening ceremonies, the Olympic gymnastics competition began. And the long awaited confrontation between Nadia and Olga was finally about to happen.

On the floor of the Montreal Forum the beam and uneven bars stood at either end and in between them were the horse for the vault and the floor exercise mat. A large scoreboard hung over the arena. The judges' scores would be tabulated by a computer and the results flashed without the usual frustrating delay.

Sunday night the Russians and the Romanians performed at the same time. Sitting in the Forum, a spectator could see all of the biggest names in women's gymnastics working in separate events. In her early routines Olga looked tight. Coming out of a handstand in her floor exercise she toppled over and failed to finish in the top five places in that event. She recovered on her vault with a 9.75, tied for second in the balance beam with a 9.80 and did a beautiful bar routine earning a 9.90. But her high scores weren't high enough. Nadia finished ahead of Olga in the vault, floor exercise and beam.

Nadia's performance on the uneven bars was even better. She finished the routine and waited briefly for the score. The scoreboard lit up with a 1.00. There was shocked silence at first, then explosive applause as the crowd realized what had happened. Nadia had not received a 1.00 but a 10.0, a perfect 10, the first perfect score in Olympic history. No one had anticipated that any gymnast would score a 10. So when the scoreboard's computer had been programed, the highest possible score that the board could display was a 9.99. Nadia had not only won the bar event, but she had also defeated the computer.

As the optional phase of the meet began on Monday, the Soviet team was in the lead. Nadia was leading in the individual standings. Korbut began with a 9.9 on the bars, but dropped further behind in the floor exercise and vault. At the same time Nadia looked stronger than ever. On the balance beam and uneven bars she received two more perfect marks.

Probably the most exciting moment of her performance was her dismount from the uneven bars. In a forward motion she released her grip on the high bar, did a half-twist and finished the movement with a back somersault. Nadia executes this move with such consistent precision that it is called the "Salto

Comaneci." Ann Carr, a member of the U.S. Olympic team has another name for it. She calls it "madness."

Nadia's high scores could not push her team into the lead. For the seventh consecutive year the Russian women won the team gold medal. During the award ceremony, Nadia and Olga shook hands for the first time. And suddenly tickets for the remaining two gymnastics sessions were harder to get than gold medals.

If the outcome of the face-off between Comaneci and Korbut was still in doubt, Wednesday's all-around competition settled the matter. Nadia's first score of the evening was a 9.85 on the vault. Olga attacked the bars and, as some of her fans chanted "Ol-ga, Ol-ga," the judges gave her a 9.9. For a moment it seemed that Korbut might be headed for a comeback. But Nadia was making a habit of perfection. She flew through a bar routine and grabbed still another 10. Olga fought back on the balance beam. She was inspired, but somehow exceeded the time limit and had to settle for a mediocre 9.5. Olga walked away. Her defeat by Comaneci was now certain.

When the medals were awarded for the all-around competition, Nadia received the gold, Nelli Kim won the silver and Tourishcheva — once again overshadowed — took the bronze. On the awards platform, Ludmilla congratulated Nadia with a kiss. It was a gesture of simple respect but also one of recognition. Ludmilla, the former Olympic champion was indicating that her title now belonged to Nadia. Confirming her right to the title, Nadia added two more 10s in Thursday's finals and won her second and third gold medals.

The Olympic Games were first held in ancient Greece. Since then many changes have occurred. Originally women could not participate. Not only were they banned from participation, but if they were caught even watching an event they faced the death penalty. Recently women have captured the most attention in the games. In the 1976 Winter Olympics, Sheila Young, Rosi Mittermaier and Dorothy Hamill became instant celebrities.

One important feature of the ancient games has not changed. In the early Olympics, judges cast their votes and the winner was awarded a crown of leaves from the sacred olive tree. The vote of the judges meant that the winner had achieved *arete* — the Greek word for perfection. In the Montreal Olympics, Nadia Comaneci demonstrated that she is a very modern athlete performing in a very ancient tradition.

superstars! superstars superstars superstars

CREATIVE EDUCATION SPORTS SUPERSTARS

Football
Johnny Unitas
Bob Griese
Vince Lombardi
Joe Namath
O. J. Simpson
Fran Tarkenton
Roger Staubach
Alan Page
Larry Csonka
Don Shula
Franco Harris
Terry Bradshaw
Chuck Foreman

Baseball
Frank Robinson
Tom Seaver
Jackie Robinson
Johnny Bench
Hank Aaron
Roberto Clemente
Mickey Mantle
Rod Carew
Fred Lynn
Pete Rose

Basketball
Walt Frazier
Kareem Abdul Jabbar
Wilt Chamberlain
Jerry West
Bill Russell
Bill Walton
Bob McAdoo
Julius Erving
John Havlicek
Rick Barry
George McGinnis

Tennis
Jimmy Connors
Chris Evert
Pancho Gonzales
Evonne Goolagong
Arthur Ashe
Billie Jean King
Stan Smith

Racing
Peter Revson
Jackie Stewart
A. J. Foyt
Richard Petty

Miscellaneous
Mark Spitz
Muhammad Ali
Secretariat
Olga Korbut
Evel Knievel
Jean Claude Killy
Janet Lynn
Peggy Fleming
Pelé
Rosi Mittermaier
Sheila Young
Dorothy Hamill
Nadia Comaneci

Golf
Lee Trevino
Jack Nicklaus
Arnold Palmer
Johnny Miller
Kathy Whitworth
Laura Baugh

Hockey
Phil and Tony Esposito
Gordie Howe
Bobby Hull
Bobby Orr